WITHDRAWN

D0471527

A TRUE BOOK™

My United States

Puerto Rico

NEL YOMTOV

Children's Press®
An Imprint of Scholastic Inc.

CARSON CITY LIBRARY
900 North Roop Street
Carson City, NV 89701
775-887-2244   NOV 2 1 2018

Content Consultant

James Wolfinger, PhD, Associate Dean and Professor
College of Education, DePaul University, Chicago, Illinois

Library of Congress Cataloging-in-Publication Data
Names: Yomtov, Nelson, author.
Title: Puerto Rico / by Nel Yomtov.
Description: New York : Children's Press, [2018] | Series: A true book | Includes bibliographical references and index.
Identifiers: LCCN 2017048741| ISBN 9780531235775 (library binding) | ISBN   9780531250907 (pbk.)
Subjects: LCSH: Puerto Rico—Juvenile literature
Classification: LCC F1958.3 .Y66 2018 | DDC 972.95—dc23
LC record available at https://lccn.loc.gov/2017048741

Photographs ©: Photos ©: cover: Wendell Metzen/Getty Images; back cover bottom: Keiji Iwai/Getty Images; back cover ribbon: AliceLiddelle/Getty Images; 3 bottom: Nicholas Pitt/Alamy Images; 3 map: Jim McMahon/Mapman ®; 4 left: Tom Hadley/Alamy Images; 4 right: Wolfgang Kaehler/Getty Images; 5 top: felixairphoto/iStockphoto; 5 bottom: Photo File/Getty Images; 6 bottom: honglouwawa/Getty Images; 7 bottom: Hemis/Superstock, Inc.; 7 top: dennisvdw/iStockphoto; 7 center: dennisvdw/iStockphoto; 8-9: felixairphoto/iStockphoto; 11: Stephanie Maze/Getty Images; 12: Nick Hanna/Alamy Images; 13: AFP Contributor/Getty Images; 14: Eva Parey/age fotostock; 15: dlrz4114/iStockphoto; 16-17: dennisvdw/iStockphoto; 19: Nicholas Pitt/Alamy Images; 22 left: chelovek/iStockphoto; 22 right: Darth_Vector/Shutterstock; 23 bottom left: Image Quest Marine/Alamy Images; 23 top right: Wolfgang Kaehler/Getty Images; 23 bottom right: Luiz Claudio Marigo/Minden Pictures; 23 top left: Tom Hadley/Alamy Images; 24-25: Franz Marc Frei/Getty Images; 27: Linda Whitwam/Getty Images; 29: For Alan/Alamy Images; 30 bottom left: Mary Evans/Grenville Collins/The Image Works; 30 top: De Agostini/A. Dagli Orti/Getty Images; 30 bottom right: Stock Montage/Getty Images; 31 top left: topseller/Shutterstock; 31 bottom: Darth_Vector/Shutterstock; 31 top right: Alex Wroblewski/Getty Images; 32: Alex Wroblewski/Getty Images; 33: Gladys Vega/Getty Images; 34-35: Marina Movschowitz/Alamy Images; 36: Anthony Causi/Getty Images; 37: Robert Fried/Alamy Images; 38: David R. Frazier Photolibrary, Inc./Alamy Images; 39: Carlos Giusti/AP Images; 40 inset: PhotoCuisine RM/Alamy Images; 40 background: PepitoPhotos/Getty Images; 41: John McConnico/AP Images; 42 bottom: J. Scott Applewhite/AP Images; 42 top: Everett Collection Inc/Alamy Images; 43 top left: James Dugan/Alamy Images; 43 top right: Photo File/Getty Images; 43 bottom: Scott Gries/Getty Images; 44 bottom: Geilynet Montalvo/EyeEm/Getty Images; 44 top: Per Bengtsson/Shutterstock; 44 center left: imagedb.com/Shutterstock; 44 center right: dennisvdw/iStockphoto; 45 center: CTK/Alamy Images; 45 top right: Rad K/Shutterstock; 45 top left: A Bello/Exactostock-1598/Superstock, Inc.; 45 bottom: dennisvdw/iStockphoto.

Maps by Map Hero, Inc.

No part of this publication may be reproduced in whole or in part, or stored in a retrieval system, or transmitted in any form or by any means, electronic, mechanical, photocopying, recording, or otherwise, without written permission of the publisher. For information regarding permission, write to Scholastic Inc., Attention: Permissions Department, 557 Broadway, New York, NY 10012.
© 2019 Scholastic Inc.

All rights reserved. Published in 2019 by Children's Press, an imprint of Scholastic Inc.
Printed in North Mankato, MN, USA 113

SCHOLASTIC, CHILDREN'S PRESS, A TRUE BOOK™, and associated logos are trademarks and/or registered trademarks of Scholastic Inc.

Scholastic Inc., 557 Broadway, New York, NY 10012

1 2 3 4 5 6 7 8 9 10 R 28 27 26 25 24 23 22 21 20 19

Front cover: Old San Juan

Back cover: Dolphin

Welcome to Puerto Rico

Find the Truth!

Everything you are about to read is true **except** for one of the sentences on this page.

Which one is **TRUE**?

T or F Puerto Ricans are U.S. citizens.

T or F Puerto Rico is a U.S. state.

UNITED STATES

Puerto Rico

PUERTO RICO
BOI 894
Isla Del Encanto

Find the answers in this book.

3

Contents

Puerto Rican hibiscus

THE **BIG** TRUTH!

What Represents Puerto Rico?

Stripe-headed tanager

Cayo Luis Peña

Roberto Clemente

This Is Puerto Rico!

N W E S

0 20 Miles

ATLANTIC OCEAN

1 Arecibo Observatory

1 Arecibo Lighthouse and Historical Park

San Cristóbal Fort

Old San Juan
2 SAN JUAN

3 El Yunque National Forest

Culebra Island

ARECIBO

BAYAMÓN

Manatí

La Plata

Loíza

CAROLINA

4 →

Caguana Indian Ceremonial Park

Arecibo

Añasco

MAYAGÜEZ

CAGUAS

Vieques Passage

Vieques Sound

Mona Passage

PUERTO RICO

Tres Picachos

Central Mountains

Vieques Island

PONCE

Caja de Muertos

Las Cabezas de San Juan State Park

Cartagena Lagoon Natural Reserve

Ponce Museum of Art

Parque de Las Ciencias Luis A. Ferré

Cabo Rojo Lighthouse

1 Arecibo Observatory

Located in northwestern Puerto Rico, this observatory contains one of the world's largest radio telescopes. It was the first telescope used to detect planets beyond our solar system.

② Old San Juan

Along the cobblestone streets of the capital city's colonial section, modern shops sit beside 500-year-old forts and churches. World-class museums celebrate the history and culture of the "Island of Enchantment."

③ El Yunque National Forest

Covering more than 28,000 acres (11,331 hectares), this natural wonder is the only tropical rain forest in the U.S. National Forest System. Many ancient Taíno rock carvings are located along the Icacos River within the forest.

VIRGIN I
(U.I

VIRGIN ISLANDS
(U.S.)

An

St. M

④ Culebra National Wildlife Refuge

Established in 1909, this wildlife reserve covers the island of Culebra and 23 small islands nearby. It is home to dozens of species of plants, birds, and reptiles.

CARIBBEAN
SEA

Cayo Luis Peña is one of many uninhabited islands that are a part of Puerto Rico.

CHAPTER 1

Land and Wildlife

Puerto Rico is famous for its sparkling beaches, tropical rain forests, and warm climate. Its rich history and modern bustling cities attract visitors from around the world. The sound of the Spanish language fills the air. Puerto Rico is not a state, nor is it an independent country. It is a possession of the United States called a **commonwealth**. Yet to many people, including Puerto Ricans themselves, this friendly place is best described as the Island of Enchantment.

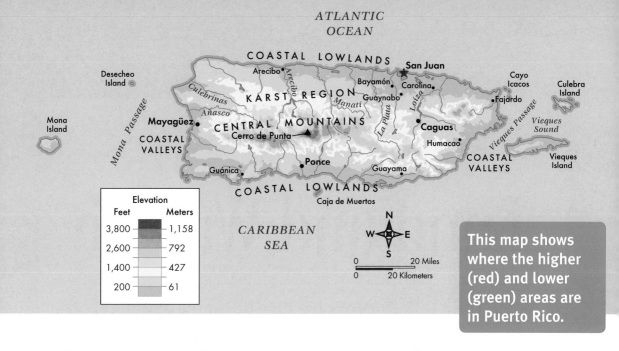

This map shows where the higher (red) and lower (green) areas are in Puerto Rico.

Mountains, Valleys, and Beaches

Puerto Rico is an **archipelago** consisting of one main island and a number of smaller ones. It is located about 1,000 miles (1,609 kilometers) southeast of the tip of Florida. To its north lies the Atlantic Ocean, and to the south lies the Caribbean Sea. The main island, which is simply called Puerto Rico, is about 90 miles (145 km) long and 30 miles (48 km) wide. The largest of the smaller islands are Vieques, Culebra, and Mona.

Deep Down Below

The Camuy Caves, located in Puerto Rico's northwestern **karst** region, is one of the biggest cave systems in the world. It was carved by the Camuy River about a million years ago. **Geologists** have so far discovered more than 200 caves spread over 10 miles (16 km). The largest of them, Clara Cave, is 700 feet (213 meters) long and 215 feet (65 m) high. That means a 20-story building could stand inside it!

Walking tours of the Camuy Caves are a popular tourist attraction.

11

Puerto Rico's highest peak is Cerro de Punta. This mountain has a height of 4,390 feet (1,338 m).

A range of tall mountains called the Cordillera Central, or Central Mountains, stretches from east to west across the middle of the island. Farmers grow crops in the rich soil of the valleys between the mountains. The karst region lies on the northern side of the mountains. This area features deep caves and underground rivers and lakes. The coastal lowlands are flat, narrow strips of land that run along Puerto Rico's north and south coasts. The island's largest cities are located in these areas.

Climate

Puerto Rico has a comfortable, warm climate. Rainfall can be heavy, especially in the lush rain forests of the eastern Central Mountains. **Hurricanes** are a frequent threat. In September 2017, Hurricanes Irma and Maria destroyed buildings and crops and knocked out electricity across the entire island. Tens of thousands of people were left displaced, without food, clean water, and fuel.

MAXIMUM TEMPERATURE
104°F

MINIMUM TEMPERATURE
40°F

During Hurricane Maria, winds blew at speeds up to 175 miles (282 km) per hour.

The roots of mangrove trees are embedded in the mud underwater.

Plants

Due to human activities and hurricane damage, most of Puerto Rico's rain forests are gone, but the island is still home to about 3,000 species of plants. Colorful flowers such as hibiscus, orchids, and jasmine grow everywhere. Green plants thrive on the hillsides and mountains. Kapok trees, bamboo, fern, and coconut palms grow throughout the islands. Mangrove swamps are found along the coasts. The long, fingerlike roots of the mangrove provide an ideal home for a variety of birds and **marine** life.

Animals

Puerto Rico is home to thousands of species of wildlife. Warblers, woodpeckers, hummingbirds, falcons, parrots, and stripe-headed tanagers soar through the skies. Lizards such as iguanas and anoles also live on the island. The coqui is a small tree frog with a loud, cheerful call. Sharks, dolphins, barracudas, manatees, and tunas swim in the island's waters. No large mammals live on Puerto Rico, but about 13 species of bats are found there.

There are more iguanas than people in Puerto Rico.

Founded in 1521, San Juan is the oldest city in the United States.

"EL DERECHO, LA LIBERTAD Y LA DIGNIDAD"
POR ENCIMA DE TODO"
LUIS MUÑOZ RIVERA

CHAPTER 2

Government

Puerto Rico's capitol in San Juan, El Capitolio, was built in 1929. The idea for building a capitol was first introduced in 1907, but construction did not begin until 1925. Its dome was added in 1961. Located in an area called Old San Juan, the three-story structure stands 147 feet (45 m) high. The original copy of Puerto Rico's **constitution** is displayed on the main floor of the building.

Commonwealth Government Basics

Like the U.S. government, the government of Puerto Rico is divided into three branches: executive, legislative, and judicial. The governor is the head of the executive branch. The legislative branch, made up of the Senate and the House of Representatives, creates Puerto Rico's laws. The judicial branch is a system of courts that hear cases and decide how the commonwealth's laws are put into effect.

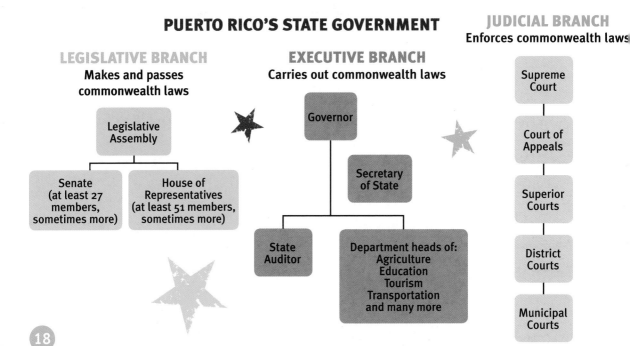

PUERTO RICO'S STATE GOVERNMENT

LEGISLATIVE BRANCH
Makes and passes
commonwealth laws

Legislative Assembly

Senate (at least 27 members, sometimes more)

House of Representatives (at least 51 members, sometimes more)

EXECUTIVE BRANCH
Carries out commonwealth laws

Governor

Secretary of State

State Auditor

Department heads of:
Agriculture
Education
Tourism
Transportation
and many more

JUDICIAL BRANCH
Enforces commonwealth laws

Supreme Court

Court of Appeals

Superior Courts

District Courts

Municipal Courts

The Commonwealth at Work

In Puerto Rico, voters and local officials make decisions about local matters, such as education, transportation, and public

Puerto Rico's local government is responsible for law enforcement and other public services.

health. Government business is conducted mostly in Spanish. The U.S. government is responsible for the island's defense, foreign relations, communications, and all other things it oversees for individual states. Puerto Ricans are U.S. citizens, but they cannot vote to elect the U.S. president. They can elect a representative to the U.S. Congress, but he or she has no vote. Because they have no voice in the U.S. government, Puerto Ricans do not pay federal income taxes.

A Question of Status

Puerto Ricans are divided on the issue of their island's political status. Should it become an independent country or a state, or should it remain a commonwealth? Some people think independence could harm the island's economy. Residents might also lose their U.S. citizenship and the right to live and work in the United States. On the other hand, independence would give Puerto Ricans more control over the government decisions that affect them. Becoming the 51st state would mean residents would have to pay U.S. federal income taxes. The island, however, would gain U.S. voting rights and true representation in Congress.

The People of Puerto Rico

Elected officials in Puerto Rico represent a population with a range of interests and lifestyles.

Ethnicity (2016 estimates)

99%

Hispanic
or Latino

1%
Other

24.2% of the population has a college degree.

2.8% of Puerto Ricans were born in other countries.

73% have graduated from high school.

5.5% speak English at home. Spanish is the most common language used in the commonwealth.

68.9% own their own homes.

21

What Represents Puerto Rico?

Puerto Rico has chosen specific animals, plants, and objects to represent the values and characteristics of the land and its people. Find out why these symbols were chosen to represent Puerto Rico or discover surprising curiosities about them.

Seal

The castles, lions, and flags in the outer circle of the seal represent the Spanish kingdoms that made Puerto Rico a **colony**. The green circle represents the island's plant life. The gold letters *F* and *I* stand for "Ferdinand" and "Isabella," who were the king and queen of Spain when Spanish explorers arrived in Puerto Rico. The Latin-language motto means "John is his name," which refers to John the Baptist, the patron saint of Puerto Rico.

Flag

Puerto Rico's flag was officially adopted in 1952. It was inspired by the flag of Cuba. The white star stands for the commonwealth. The blue triangle and the three red stripes represent the three branches of Puerto Rico's government. The two white stripes stand for human and individual rights.

Stripe-Headed Tanager

OFFICIAL BIRD

Tanagers have a black head with two white stripes, one above the eyes and one below the eyes. Males have a bright orange chest and neck, while females are a dull olive-green color.

Puerto Rican Hibiscus

OFFICIAL FLOWER

This flower of the maga tree thrives in tropical climates and is treasured for its attractive pink or white petals.

Coqui

OFFICIAL ANIMAL

Measuring 1 to 2 inches (2.5 to 5 centimeters) long, this beloved tree frog is named for its loud nighttime call, "ko-KEE, ko-KEE!" Unlike many frogs, coquis don't have webbed feet. They have special toe pads that help them cling to trees and leaves.

Kapok

OFFICIAL TREE

The kapok can grow as much as 13 feet (4 m) a year, reaching a maximum height of about 200 feet (61 m). Kapok trees do not bloom every year. Some may go 10 years without producing flowers.

23

Just outside the town of Isabela, a stone monument honors Cacique Mabodamaca, a leader of the Taíno people during the 16th century.

CHAPTER **3**

History

Some experts believe the earliest residents of Puerto Rico came by raft from present-day Mexico. Others claim that Native Americans from Central America walked to the island. Thousands of years ago, the water level of the Caribbean Sea was lower, and people may have crossed a land bridge that connected Central America to the islands of the Caribbean. In any case, it is likely that humans first arrived on Puerto Rico about 9,000 years ago.

Native Americans

The earliest inhabitants of Puerto Rico were the Casimiroid and Saladoid peoples, who came from the northeastern coast of South America. The Arawak people from modern-day Venezuela and Brazil arrived in Puerto Rico around 800 CE. The group of Arawak people who settled in Puerto Rico are called the Taíno. For centuries, the Taíno were the only people in Puerto Rico. Another group, the Carib, also came from South America and began settling in the area in the late 1400s.

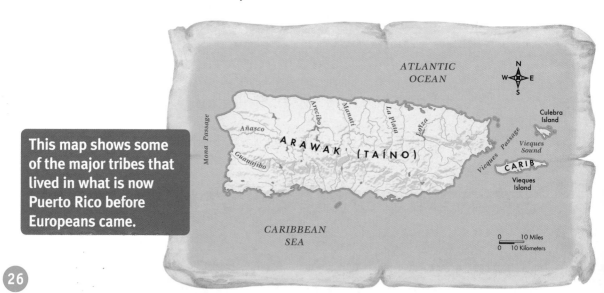

This map shows some of the major tribes that lived in what is now Puerto Rico before Europeans came.

At Tibes Indigenous Ceremonial Center in south-central Puerto Rico, archaeologists discovered many remains and artifacts of the Taíno people. Today, the site is an educational center showing how the Taíno lived.

The Taíno built houses with thatched roofs, called *bohíos*. They hunted, fished, and planted crops. Local chiefs called *caciques* ruled Taíno villages. The Taíno traveled between Puerto Rico and nearby islands in large canoes carved from the trunks of kapok trees. A peaceful people, the Taíno enjoyed a ball game called *batey*, which was played on long courts.

27

The Europeans Arrive

In 1493, Christopher Columbus, sailing from Spain, landed on Puerto Rico during his second voyage to America. He named the island San Juan Bautista and returned home. In 1508, Spanish **conquistador** Juan Ponce de León arrived on the island to establish a colony. With their horses, guns, and armor, the Spaniards quickly enslaved the Taíno and forced them to mine for gold and farm the land. Thousands of native people were killed or died from diseases the Europeans brought with them.

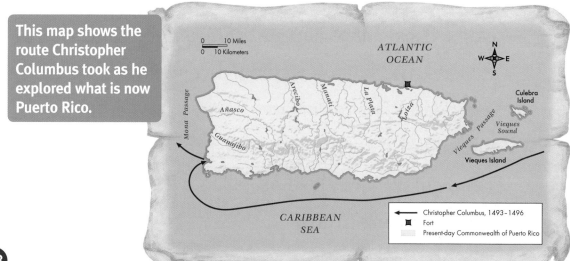

This map shows the route Christopher Columbus took as he explored what is now Puerto Rico.

A group of Puerto Ricans poses for a photo on a plantation.

By 1550, Spain had established a powerful empire in the Caribbean islands and many parts of Central and South America. Gold, silver, and plantations that grew sugarcane, cotton, and coffee had made the Spaniards wealthy. Enslaved African people were made to clear trees and work the plantations. Many Puerto Rican farmers began growing crops not to profit Spain, but themselves. They traded with other countries, which helped the Puerto Rican economy grow.

The Quest for Independence

By the 1860s, tensions grew between Puerto Ricans and Spaniards, who still controlled the government. Many Puerto Ricans were *criollos*—people of Spanish heritage who were born in Latin America. In September 1868, several hundred people took over the farming town of Lares and declared Puerto Rico an independent state. The revolt was crushed, but the Spaniards began to grant the criollos more freedoms.

Timeline of Puerto Rico Events

ca. 800 CE
The Arawak people begin arriving.

1508
Ponce de León arrives to establish a Spanish colony.

7000 BCE > **800 CE** > **1493** > **1508**

ca. 7000 BCE
People come to Puerto Rico for the first time.

1493
Christopher Columbus lands on Puerto Rico.

The United States Takes Over

In 1898, war broke out between the United States and Spain. U.S. troops invaded Puerto Rico and quickly won the conflict. Spain gave control of the island to the United States, which set up a military government. This government allowed U.S. corporations to take over most of the island's land to grow sugarcane. Small landowners were displaced, and Puerto Rico's middle class was crushed.

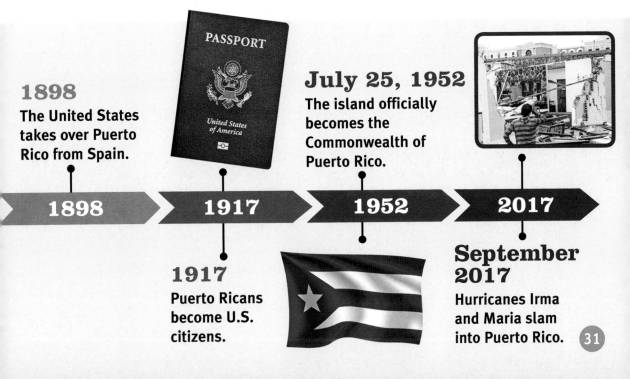

1898
The United States takes over Puerto Rico from Spain.

July 25, 1952
The island officially becomes the Commonwealth of Puerto Rico.

1898 **1917** **1952** **2017**

1917
Puerto Ricans become U.S. citizens.

September 2017
Hurricanes Irma and Maria slam into Puerto Rico.

31

Maria was the fifth-strongest hurricane ever to strike the United States.

Puerto Rico Today

In 1952, Puerto Rico officially became a commonwealth. Some Puerto Ricans were angered. They wanted complete independence. In protest, violent acts in Puerto Rico and the United States have sometimes occurred. Political status is not the only challenge facing Puerto Ricans today. The economy remains weak, and unemployment is high. Worse yet, the hurricanes in September 2017 caused billions of dollars in damage. Experts predict it will take years to fully restore the island.

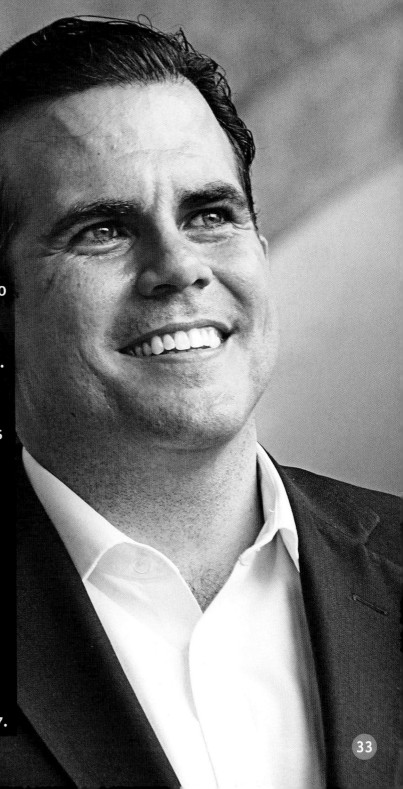

Ricardo Antonio Rosselló: Governor for Statehood

The son of former Puerto Rico governor Pedro Rosselló, Ricardo Antonio Rosselló was born in San Juan in 1979. After earning a doctorate from the University of Michigan, he entered politics and was elected the 12th governor of Puerto Rico in 2016. Rosselló strongly supports statehood for Puerto Rico and the right of Puerto Ricans to elect representatives to the U.S. Congress. As governor, he worked to improve the economy and helped his homeland recover from the damaging hurricanes of 2017.

Bomba and plena are heavily rhythmic forms of music that originated in Puerto Rico.

CHAPTER 4

Culture

Puerto Rico's visual arts and crafts have been shaped by Native American, African, and Spanish traditions. Festival masks and ornately designed hammocks are a blend of African and Spanish styles. José Campeche, Francisco Oller, and Myrna Báez are well-known Puerto Rican painters whose works have been displayed in museums around the world. The Museum of Art of Puerto Rico in San Juan is a world-class museum and a favorite tourist spot.

Sports and Recreation

Baseball is the national sport of Puerto Rico. The island has produced more than 200 Major League Baseball players, including superstars Roberto Clemente, Iván Rodríguez, Yadier Molina, and Francisco Lindor. Puerto Rico has also been the home of about 60 world champion boxers, including Miguel Cotto and Amanda Serrano. Puerto Rico's national basketball team has participated in nine Olympic Games.

Puerto Rico's baseball team celebrates a home run in a game against the Dominican Republic.

The Luis A. Ferré Performing Arts Center in San Juan hosts concerts, ballets, and other performances.

A Festival of Music

Puerto Rico celebrates many historical events and religious holidays, including Constitution Day, Three Kings Day, and Christmas. Since 1956, Puerto Ricans have held a classical music event in honor of the famous cellist Pablo Casals. Born in Spain, Casals moved to Puerto Rico, his mother's homeland, in the 1950s. The Casals Festival has become the number one musical event in the Caribbean. Dozens of first-rate musicians from around the world come to perform each year.

Workers package medications at a factory in Puerto Rico.

What People Do

Puerto Ricans work in a wide range of businesses. Many Puerto Ricans work in factories that make medications and electronics. More than 250,000 Puerto Ricans work for the government. Others work in industries such as sales, construction, health care, tourism, and transportation. Once an important industry, agriculture today employs few people. And its future does not look bright: The hurricanes of 2017 destroyed nearly 80 percent of Puerto Rico's agriculture industry.

21st-Century Farming

In 2015, Puerto Rico imported more than 85 percent of its produce. With agriculture in decline, some farmers have begun to use **drones** to scout possible new growing areas and to check the health of their existing crops. Growers have also set up websites where people can buy produce directly from Puerto Rican farmers. Farmers pack the food, and it is delivered the next day to the 50 states and within Puerto Rico.

A market in San Juan displays locally grown produce for sale.

Good Eats!

Arroz con gandules, or pigeon peas and rice seasoned with sweet chili peppers, is one of Puerto Rico's favorite dishes. It can be served alone or with side dishes like *pollo guisado,* or chicken stew, and a salad. People also enjoy **plantains**, either eaten alone or served with rice or meat stews.

 ## Green Banana Salad

 Ask an adult to help you!

This hearty, healthy salad is popular throughout Puerto Rico as a side dish.

Ingredients

6 small unripe (green) bananas, unpeeled
2 cups shrimp, peeled
1 tablespoon olive oil
1 green bell pepper, sliced into rings

1 sweet onion, finely chopped
2 slices crisp, cooked bacon, crumbled
White vinegar
Brown sugar

Directions

Cook the bananas in boiling water until tender. Remove the peels. Cut into small chunks and place in a large bowl. In a large skillet over medium-high heat, cook the shrimp in the oil. Add the cooked shrimp, bell pepper, and onion to the bananas in the bowl. Sprinkle on the bacon and season the salad with vinegar and sugar.

Each September, people gather in the town of Lares to celebrate the anniversary of an 1868 revolt against Spanish colonizers.

Commonwealth at a Crossroads

Puerto Rico's future is uncertain. Hurricanes have destroyed roads, homes, and businesses. Water systems and power lines need to be rebuilt. But there is hope. Businesses, government, and the Puerto Rican people know they must join together to rebuild and renew the scenic Island of Enchantment. Puerto Rico's people have overcome great obstacles throughout their history, and this time is sure to be no different. ★

Famous People

Pedro Albizu Campos

(1891–1965), a native of Ponce, was a leading voice in the fight for Puerto Rican independence. His efforts were sometimes marked by violence, and he served more than 20 years in prison. He was the first Puerto Rican graduate of Harvard University.

Rafael Carrión Sr.

(1891–1964), born in San Juan, helped found Banco Popular de Puerto Rico, the largest bank in Puerto Rico and the largest Hispanic bank in the United States. The Carrión family has run the bank since it was founded in 1923.

Julia de Burgos

(1914–1953) was a poet and activist who argued in favor of Puerto Rican independence. She was born in the town of Carolina.

Sister Isolina Ferré Aguayo

(1914–2000) was a Ponce native who used her family's influence and wealth to establish schools, hospitals, and youth centers in Puerto Rico, New York City, and the eastern United States. Known as the "Mother Teresa of Puerto Rico," she was awarded the Presidential Medal of Freedom for her humanitarian work.

Roberto Clemente

(1934–1972) was a Major League Baseball star from Carolina who played his entire 18-year career with the Pittsburgh Pirates. He won 12 Gold Glove Awards and was named to 15 All-Star teams. In 1966, he won the National League Most Valuable Player Award. He died in a plane crash while attempting to deliver supplies to earthquake victims in Nicaragua.

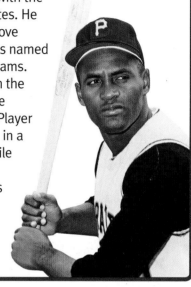

Ricardo E. Alegría

(1921–2011) pioneered the study of the Taíno people in Puerto Rico. Born in San Juan, he helped found the Institute of Puerto Rican Culture, an archaeological park established to preserve and teach the island's rich heritage.

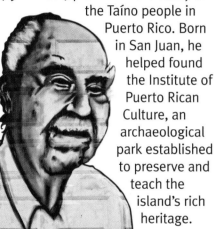

Antonia Novello

(1944–), a native of Fajardo, was the first woman and the first Hispanic to serve as U.S. surgeon general. She focused her efforts on women's and children's health and on alcohol and tobacco use by teenagers.

Georgina Lázaro-Leon

(1965–), born in San Juan, is a poet whose work introduces children to important writers, playwrights, and other figures of Hispanic culture. Several singers and composers have recorded her poems and lullabies.

Did You Know That ...

The name *Puerto Rico* ("rich port" in Spanish) is thought to come from the large amounts of gold the Spaniards found on the island.

Puerto Rico is a coffee lover's dream come true: There are more than 4,000 coffee farms on the island.

Puerto Rico is about the size of Connecticut and is one of the most densely populated islands in the world.

The streets of Old San Juan are paved with shimmering blue cobblestones.

"La Borinqueña" is the national anthem of Puerto Rico. The title comes from the Taíno name for the island, *Borinkén*. This name means "land of the brave lord."

San Juan is home to two of the oldest churches in the Americas. The Church of San José was built in the 1530s, while San Juan Cathedral was built in 1540.

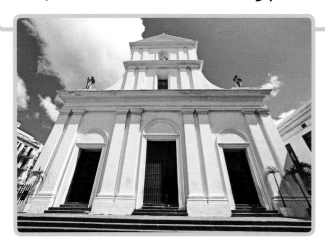

Because Puerto Rico is a territory of the United States, Americans do not need a passport to travel there, even though it can only be reached by airplane or boat from the mainland United States.

Puerto Rico has competed in the Olympic Games since 1948. In 2016, tennis player Monica Puig won Puerto Rico's first gold medal.

Did you find the truth?

 T Puerto Ricans are U.S. citizens.

 F Puerto Rico is a U.S. state.

Resources

Books

Bjorklund, Ruth, and Richard Hantula. *Puerto Rico: The Island of Enchantment.* New York: Cavendish Square, 2016.

Yasuda, Anita. *What's Great About Puerto Rico?* Minneapolis: Lerner Publications, 2015.

Visit this Scholastic website for more information on Puerto Rico:
★ www.factsfornow.scholastic.com
Enter the keywords **Puerto Rico**

Important Words

archipelago (ahr-kuh-PEL-uh-goh) a group of islands

colony (KAH-luh-nee) a territory that has been settled by people from another country and is controlled by that country

commonwealth (KAH-muhn-welth) a nation or state that is governed by the people who live there

conquistador (kahn-KEE-stuh-dor) a Spanish soldier and explorer who used violence and other methods to conquer foreign lands

constitution (kahn-stih-TOO-shuhn) the basic laws of a state, commonwealth, or country that state the rights of the people and the powers of the government

drones (DROHNZ) aircraft without a pilot that are controlled remotely

geologists (jee-AH-luh-jists) people who study Earth's physical structure

hurricanes (HUR-uh-kainz) violent storms with heavy rain and high winds

karst (KARST) terrain with rocky ground, caves, and underground rivers

marine (muh-REEN) having to do with the ocean

plantains (PLAN-tinz) tropical fruits that look like bananas but are usually eaten cooked

Index

Page numbers in **bold** indicate illustrations.

About the Author

Nel Yomtov is an award-winning author who has written nonfiction books and graphic novels about American and world history, geography, science, mythology, sports, science, careers, and country studies. He is a frequent contributor to Scholastic book series.